Insect Families

by Lisa Trumbauer

STECK-VAUGHN

Harcourt Supplemental Publishers

www.steck-vaughn.com

CONTENTS

All in the Insect Family

Go outside on a warm summer day. Look around. What insects do you see? You might see bees and butterflies flying from flower to flower. You might see ants scurrying across the sidewalk. You might see ladybugs crawling on leaves.

Bees, butterflies, ants, wasps, and ladybugs all look different. But they are all insects. And all insects are alike in some ways.

All insects each have six legs. All insects each have three body parts. They have a head, a **thorax,** and an **abdomen.**

All insects have an **exoskeleton.** This is a hard covering on the outside of their bodies. Most insects have **antennas.** Most insects also have wings and hatch from eggs.

antenna

head

thorax

wing

leg

abdomen

5

There are more than a million kinds of insects. While each kind of insect is different from any other kind, some have things in common. Different kinds of insects that have things in common are said to be in the same insect family.

Take a look at these insects—an ant, a bee, and a wasp. What do you notice? You can see the three parts of each insect's body—the head, the thorax, and the abdomen. Wasps, bees, and ants are in the same insect family.

Ant

Wasp

Bee

Many of the insects in this family
have wings. They also have mouths
that chew and bite. Bees have a
special mouth part that helps them
drink **nectar** from flowers. Many
of these insects also have stingers
at the end of their abdomens.

Wasp stinger

Ant mouth

Flying wasp

Most ants, bees, and wasps live in large groups. They build their own homes. Ants dig tunnels. Bees build beehives. Wasps build nests.

Ant tunnel

Wasp nest

Beehive

Ants, bees, and wasps all lay eggs. A **larva** hatches from each egg. It looks like a small worm. The larva will turn into a **pupa.** The pupa will turn into an adult insect.

LIFE CYCLE OF A BEE

Egg

Larva

Pupa

Adult

What a Pest!

Have you ever eaten outside and been bothered by flies? Or have you played outdoors at night and been bitten by mosquitoes?

Flies and mosquitoes belong to the same insect family. Both of these insects have two wings. Each wing is attached to one side of the thorax.

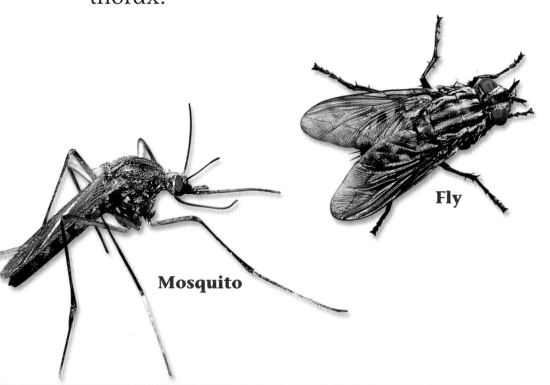

Mosquito

Fly

The larva of a fly is called a maggot.

Like bees, ants, and wasps, flies and mosquitoes change as they grow. Adult flies lay eggs. A larva hatches from each egg. The larva will turn into a pupa. The pupa will turn into an adult fly.

LIFE CYCLE OF A FLY

Egg

Larva

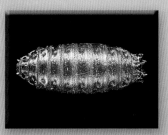
Pupa

Adult

Mosquitoes lay their eggs in the water. The larvas that hatch from the eggs live in the water. They are called **wrigglers.** Fish may eat the wrigglers before the wrigglers can become adult mosquitoes.

Fish eating a wriggler

Wriggler

Moths and butterflies can be very beautiful. Both kinds of insects have two pairs of wings. The wings are covered in tiny scales.

Butterflies and moths change as they grow. The larvas of butterflies and moths are called caterpillars.

Moth

Butterfly

Scales on a butterfly wing

Butterflies and moths seem alike, but they are different in some ways. A butterfly has colorful wings. Moth wings are usually dull.

A butterfly rests with its wings upright. A moth rests with its wings out to the sides.

Butterfly

Moth

Both butterflies and moths have antennas. But their antennas are not the same shape. A butterfly's antennas are thin and straight. A moth's antennas are wide and feathery.

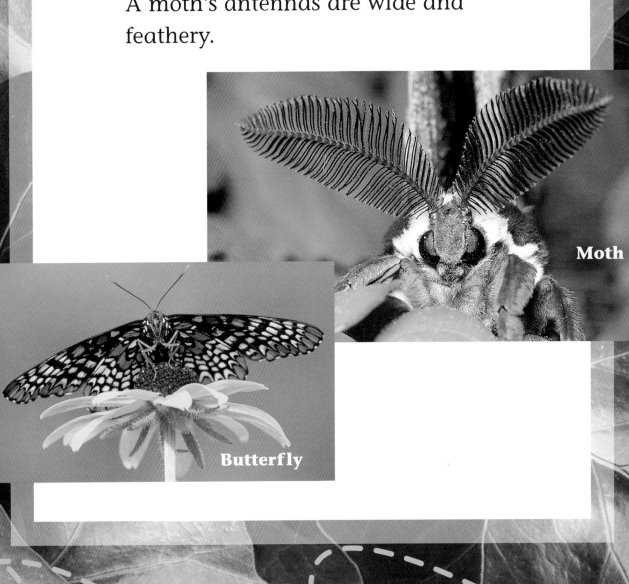

Moth

Butterfly

Butterflies and moths both have a special mouth part that is shaped like a long tube. It helps them drink nectar from flowers.

Moth drinking nectar

Hard Outer Shells

Beetles make up the largest insect family. There are about 250,000 different kinds of beetles! You probably have seen some kinds of beetles. Did you know that ladybugs are beetles? Fireflies are beetles, too!

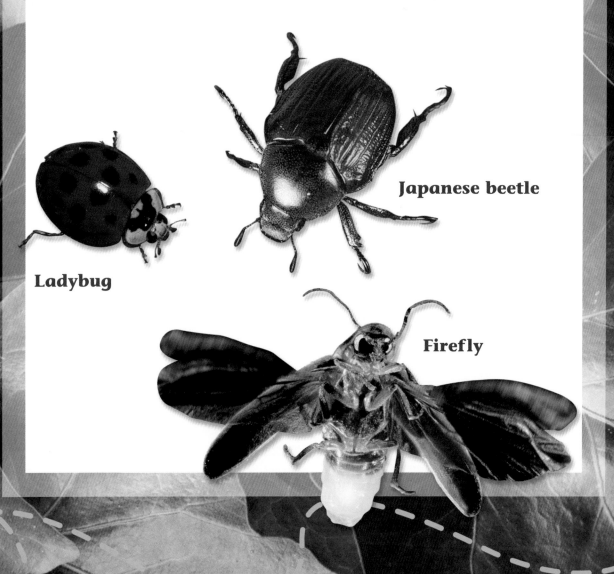

Japanese beetle

Ladybug

Firefly

All beetles have a special wing covering. The covering is actually a pair of wings. These "covering" wings protect the flying wings underneath. They act like a hard outer shell.

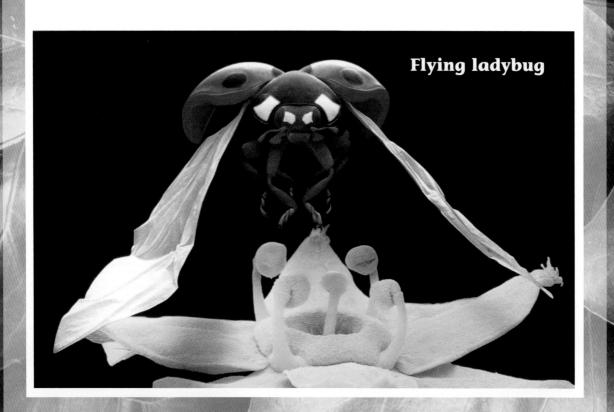

Flying ladybug

Beetles come in all shapes and sizes. Some beetles are very small. Ladybugs are one kind of small beetle. Other beetles are huge! A kind of beetle called the Hercules beetle can be more than six inches long!

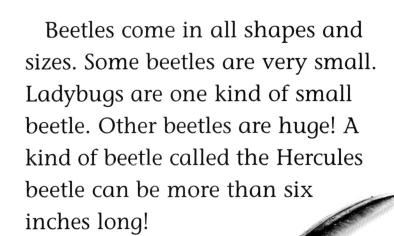

Ladybug

Hercules beetle

Beetles also change as they grow. Larvas hatch from eggs and turn into pupas. The adult insect comes out of the pupa.

Beetles live in most parts of the world. Water beetles even live in the water!

LIFE CYCLE OF A LADYBUG

Egg

Larva

Pupa

Adult

Look at the grasshopper and the cricket. What do you notice? Both insects have long back legs. These back legs are great for jumping. All of the insects in this family are really good jumpers. Many of these insects also have wings.

Grasshopper

Cricket

These insects change as they grow, too. But they only have three stages in their life cycle. The adult lays eggs, usually in the ground or in a plant. A **nymph** hatches from the egg.

LIFE CYCLE OF A GRASSHOPPER

Egg

Nymph

Adult

Grasshoppers are active during the day. Crickets are active at night.

A nymph looks like an adult, but it doesn't have wings. The nymph will grow. It will shed its skin. Later, it will turn into an adult insect and grow wings.

Nymph shedding its skin

Most grasshoppers and crickets can make noise. Some make noise by rubbing their wings together. Others make sounds by rubbing their legs against their bodies.

Usually only the male insect makes a sound. He does this to find a female insect.

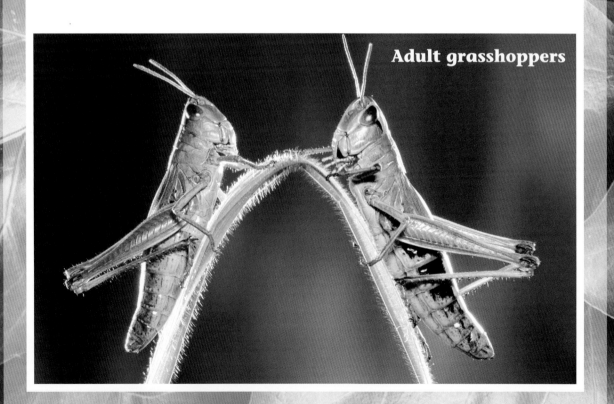

Adult grasshoppers

Like a Fairy Tale

Dragonflies and damselflies sound like characters in a fairy tale. But they are really members of another insect family! These insects have long bodies and long wings. The have very big eyes and very short antennas.

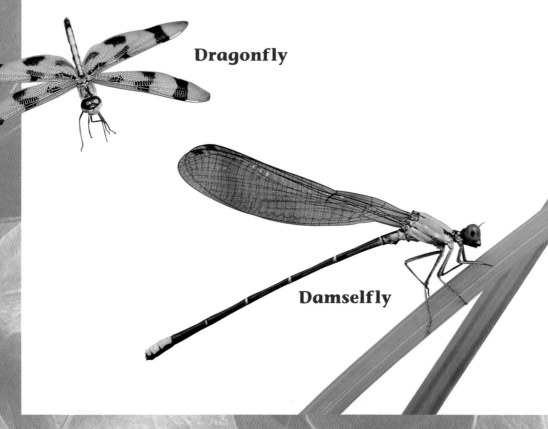

Dragonfly

Damselfly

What else do you notice about the bodies of these insects? Their legs are very close to their bodies. Short legs help the insects hold on to plants.

Dragonfly

Like grasshoppers and crickets, dragonflies and damselflies have only three stages in their life cycle. Most dragonflies and damselflies lay their eggs in water. Nymphs hatch from the eggs. The nymphs grow into adult insects.

LIFE CYCLE OF A DRAGONFLY

Egg

Adult

Nymph

Dragonflies lived 270 million years ago. Their wings were over 2 feet long.

Dragonflies and damselflies live near water. They are important to life in ponds, lakes, and streams. The nymphs eat many small creatures. The adults eat other insects, such as mosquitoes.

Damselflies

Which Is Which?

Our world is filled with insects. They are interesting creatures. Each has its own special features. Do you remember which insects belong to the same family?

GLOSSARY

abdomen
the third part of an insect's body, the part farthest from the head

antennas
long feelers on the head of an insect

exoskeleton
the hard, outside covering of an insect's body

larva
an early stage in the life cycle of an insect when it looks like a worm

nectar
liquid in flowers that insects drink

nymph
a stage in the life cycle of some insects before they become adults

pupa
the middle stage in the life cycle of some insects

thorax
the middle part of an insect's body

wrigglers
the larvas of mosquitoes